D1093019

10-16-72

This Cup

This Cup

Meditations on Holy Week

by Addison H. Leitch

BAKER BOOK HOUSE
Grand Rapids, Michigan

PRINTED IN THE UNITED STATES OF AMERICA

1717112

Contents

1

Gethsemane

What happened in Gethsemane reflected the inner strug-
gle of our Lord as He faced the cross. It was a struggle
against the powers of evil which confronted Him there.
It also reflects the very human agony of one who chose
death although He could have escaped with His life.
What we know of Gethsemane must have been shared
with His disciples later, but we are faced with the fact
that although He shared what happened there, He did
not share the meanings of the events. Our meditations
grow out of a search for meanings, for Him and for us.

SOME YEARS AGO the great Scotch theologian John Baillie made a very sound suggestion when he urged that in matters theological one is wise to use the expression *at least* instead of the word *only*. What he meant was that when one insists that his is the *only* Christian interpretation he will not only be narrow and overly argumentative, but will also block off for himself and others many possibly rich and instructive insights. It is better to say with regard to some Christian understanding that it is *at least* all this and maybe much more. For example, there are many views of the atonement, what transpired on the cross, what it means when we say that Christ died for our sins. The cross is an example; it has moral influence; it satisfies the requirements of God's holy law, for a ransom was paid; Christ entered the fray and defeated the evil adversary; words like *vicarious*, *substitutionary*, and *satisfaction* all have meaning and place in our understanding. In each case the truth has been spoken even though some ideas include more truth than others. But altogether all these truths are not the whole truth. The cross is *at least* an example, *at least* a satisfaction toward God or toward man—and then much more. And all the views together, all the truth expressed, still provide only an approach. Who can ever sum up conclusively all that happened in history and eternity when God Almighty engaged the "prince of the powers of the air," when the Lamb was slain "from the foundations of the world," when in some cosmic sense the whole creation began to find release from its frightful groanings, or even when in humble hearts there is known the amazing grace that brings assurance and peace? The cross of Jesus Christ is at least all this, and how much more!

There is a sense in which the whole of Christ's redemptive ministry was the way of the cross. We do not know what happened in the councils of eternity but the Gospels record clearly the events that were transpiring here below. He was constantly emptying Himself, becoming obedient unto death, "yea, the death of the cross." But this cross-way was brought to climax and intensity when Jesus went to Gethsemane and on through Gethsemane to Golgotha and victory. It was in the Garden of Gethsemane that He faced the cup, and the drinking of it. Even His closest friends and followers had no appreciation of, or sensitivity to, what our Lord was suffering there and what He sensed of the suffering that lay ahead of Him; they fell asleep. Later He told them what was said and what was happening and they have told us, but who can comprehend such things? Only as men grow up into Christ, only as they face for Christ's sake their own Gethsemanes, only as they struggle toward absolute obedience in the confusing pressures of a shifty and ambiguous world, only as they experience sin in its subtle, choking way, only then do they begin to enter into His experience. And after it has all been said in human language and explained in human categories, nothing is appropriate from us but humility and reverence. It was at least all this—but infinitely more.

In Mark's account of the garden experience, and he is usually the most vivid of the Gospel writers, we are told that Jesus "began to be greatly amazed and sore troubled" (Mark 14:33). The original language allows for even greater vividness. In Phillips' translation of the same passage we read that Jesus was "horror-stricken and desperately depressed." This was just at the threshold of the Gethsemane experience. Now the time had come; this was it. The great power of evil struck Him and almost struck Him down. The one who knew no sin was now to become sin for us; what He had been fighting against all His days now came on in strength; the struggle was for life and death, light and darkness, and the stakes were for eternal destiny. No wonder that now He was amazed and horrified at the strength, fury, and treachery of sin. How strange then our own easy-going and sophisticated attitudes toward sin!

The Mark record says that "he went forward a little and fell on the ground" (14:35). The ordeal was now only in its beginning stages and already seemed to be overpowering. Gethsemane and Calvary were all of a piece, first in awful expectation and then in bloody fulfillment; the wholeness of the experience is a continuum. And who is to say which is worse, the expectation of suffering or its actuality? Two former students of mine, in different classes and at different times gave me the same account of their experiences in submarine warfare during World War II. To tell it as one of them told it, his submarine had been "found" by a destroyer on the surface and the depth bombs were being dropped around them in the pattern for the kill. The whole submarine was dead silent, all voices had been stopped, the lights had dimmed with the stopping of the generators, and in that grey subterranean silence the men could do nothing but "sweat it out," literally! My student friend sat on a hard bench in the galley and with his head in his hands he watched and heard his own sweat drop on the steel deck "as it were great drops of blood" (cf. Luke 22:44). There is no need to talk here of "sweating blood," of even "bloody sweat." There is no blood here, and is this not merely the sweat of the brow we talk about in man's labor. Significantly Genesis speaks of the sweat of the "face"—a far cry from merely the sweat of the "brow"—the long furrowed sweaty face in haggard agony. One who has ever had his nose or mouth bloodied knows how blood sounds when it strikes the pavement. That was His agony then, His sweat hitting the ground and sounding "as it were" like great drops of blood. To return to the submarine: the expectancy of death has its own special kind of agony; the death itself might well be quick and merciful. It is given to men once to die; that is the common lot of men. It is not death so much as the manner of death, the facing of death, or how one may be enabled to face it; all this can unman us. So it was with our Lord. It was the expectancy, the horror of the lingering death which only the unknown frailty of human flesh could bring to an end. In the garden, then on the cross; it is all one experience. So in sobbing desperation He prays three times: "If it be possible, let this cup pass from me"; then He prayed on through: "nevertheless, not as I will but as thou wilt" (Matt. 26:39). He will obey all the way, for us men who have not obeyed, and who can rest our eternal hopes only on His perfect obedience.

What then were the contents of that cup which He was willing to drink to the last bitter dregs? In that cup we shall surely find at least his *physical suffering*. Normally in thinking about the cross there is the temptation to dismiss the physical and hurry on to the deeper sufferings which are surely there. This is understandable since the deepest meaning of the cross is surely bound up in the words "My *soul* is exceeding sorrowful, even unto death." One has not properly considered the cross until he has pondered the profundities of the soul struggle. That was where the last battle was fought, and won. Yet Jesus did suffer and die physically. He was hammered to the tree, He wore the crown of thorns, and even so common a thing as thirst became so dominant in His dragging experience as to force a cry from His lips. The back-breaking, muscle-tearing, lung-crushing crucifixion experience had been a diabolical invention for the very purpose of producing the maximum of suffering over the longest possible time. When the soldiers hammered the two thieves to break their legs it was in order to hasten their deaths, a death where broken legs are a mercy. There is therefore no need to minimize the physical sufferings.

Other comments on the physical sufferings of Christ have had their supporters and their audiences. Why, it has been argued, has such a fuss been made over Jesus' physical pain when equal or worse pain has been suffered by many others and often for His sake? After all, it is said, there were two other men crucified at the same time and the accounts of the Gospels treat their sufferings with almost callous indifference. More than that, thousands must have been crucified in the long and gruesome history of "man's inhumanity to man," hopeless slaves in the Roman system plus all those Christians on whom great hopes had been laid who nevertheless suffered like deaths or perished by some other cruel and lingering invention. By what neat scheme, for example, did lions tear their victims to pieces and did they dawdle at their bloody work? Why so much then of Jesus' physical sufferings?

In answer to such questions at least two things must be said. In the first place, the number of people suffering has no real relationship to the suffering of one individual; every man finally suffers alone and in his own way. We are confused by statistics, for whereas the deaths of thousands or hundreds of thousands by tragic consequences overwhelm us, and our observation of all the suffering of multitudes compounds the tragedy for us, it still remains that each individual dies his own death in his own way. Death is always unique and very personal. Thus the sufferings of Christ were uniquely His own and endless numbers of like deaths neither add to nor subtract from His own sufferings. In *All Quiet on the Western Front*, the great, touching novel of the first great war, the last page reveals that the hero of the story is killed on a day when the news media reported that all was "quiet" on the western front! In our own day the reports on Vietnam are supposed to be reassuring when we learn that "only twenty-six" were killed last week. Only twenty-six! Only one is enough for that one.

That one in this case was Jesus dying for me. And this suggests the second thing that must be said about the physical sufferings. There is something called a threshold of pain. The nervous systems of different people do indeed react differently to different painful stimuli—heat and cold, for easy examples. Boxers, football players, or horny-handed fishermen learn to withstand bruising shocks. Dentists and doctors are surprised sometimes by what some people seem to be able to take in stride. That all this may be completely psychosomatic is granted, although it remains quite mysterious. What can we guess about the threshold of pain in Jesus' case? His body had not been brutalized in any way by sin; He had never sinned against His own body, the dwelling place of the Spirit of God. As essential man His body was the perfectly tuned, unmarred, sensitive instrument of His thought and will. One can be reasonably sure that He had suffered some bodily hurt before this day, but now was to come the brutal attack, the cruel, senseless, bloody attack on the citadel of His holiness. Think about Jesus' sinless body sometime. What would it be like? Then think about a cross. The cup which He dreaded was at least physical suffering. This should not be overemphasized but we surely must not minimize its stark realism.

Then there had to be at least His *mental suffering*, the shuddering expectancy of exposure and shame. We live in a day when nudity is much too frequently accepted. From the beach to the stage the idea of modesty has fallen on hard days. But there is still in all of us that inner sensitivity which makes us recoil from being exposed to the wrong people or for the wrong reasons; there is a hardening required for a burlesque queen which is not required of an artist's model. And one is rarely ready for the way in which even a professional hospital staff takes charge of our body and bodily functions. Jesus was to be stripped and exposed, and it goes without saying that the crowd would be leering and jeering, raucous in its contempt. The experience would be almost unbearable in that day when nudity was not taken for granted. The laws governing the priests and Levites of the Old Testament did not permit them to expose even their ankles when they mounted the steps to the altar; in such a milieu Jesus was to be completely exposed. It was to be a time of blood and sweat. The natural functions of the body, of which men are always ashamed, would follow their natural course in the long hours on the cross. The ordeal for a sensitive person could be only hideous.

There is a wrong impression abroad about the size of the cross. It is usually pictured as a towering sort of thing. This can be the imagination only of those who have never known the weight of wooden beams. If Jesus carried His cross, or as some suppose, only the cross-beam, or if the healthy rugged Simon of Cyrene carried it for Him, how much could either of them really carry? Nothing surely like what is usually pictured. Thinking seriously about it one can hardly picture the top of the cross as being much more than eight feet above the ground if at least three feet had to be below ground, with the cross-bar no more than seven feet above the ground. This means that those who railed at Jesus and spit on him were facing him on almost an eye-to-eye level.

"And they sat down and watched him there," so Matthew tells us (27:36). Animals crawl away to nurse their wounds and die. Men dread being a spectacle. Some may contemplate sadly and soberly how it may be with them in their own deaths when weakness of body and nerve can combine to unman them, the shame that may accompany their passing from a life which has otherwise been brave and good. Or, one may look back with shame upon weakness occasioned by a devastating, almost fatal, sickness. But such weakness is a horrendous thought with a crowd looking on. They sat down there to watch Him die. Good show! How will He manage to carry it off? The writer to the Hebrews said that Jesus was a "gazing stock" (10:33). The Greek word is *theatrize*—it was all good theater. And the same writer said that our beloved Lord, for us men and our salvation "despised the shame" (Heb. 12:2).

There in Gethsemane He could picture the coming scene and imagine a thousand ways to escape it; but He continued to pray through to obedience. What a supreme struggle this must have been! Those who would shame Him in purposeful lewdness were the very ones for whom He came to die. They couldn't possibly be worth it; they weren't! Thus the grace of God.

There is finally no understanding of Gethsemane and the cross without some probing of the *soul struggle* which there took place. Jesus, in the last analysis, died of a broken heart, and not only in the figurative sense of those words. A case has frequently been made medically that the blood and water (serum?) which flowed from His side at the plunge of the soldier's spear indicated a profound shock which had been more than mortal flesh could bear. As Frederic W. H. Myers so vividly described it:

Desperate tides of the whole great world's anguish
Forced through the channels of a single heart.

There was laid on Him "the iniquity of us all." The one who had never sinned not only experienced sin now but experienced it so completely and intensely that He "became sin for us."

Words indeed fail here for it is impossible for us, sinners, to understand and then describe what it must be like to experience sin for the first time. However one is able to describe "original sin" theologically, it must be said, at least basically, that every individual participates from his origin in the ongoing of sin in the ongoing of his humanity. Whether this sin is a matter of inheritance, or whether it begins at the time of conception—"in sin did my mother conceive me"—or whether it is part of the immediate and continuing conditioning of a new life in a sinful family or in a sinful society, every human being moves through all his days with the deadly taint a constant discoloration of his whole life. There is death in us, dislocation, disintegration, and endless drag against better efforts and finer dreams. Every thought, every aspiration, every effort is already marred at its "origin." Coupled with this basic condition is the will to sin, and so we sin "presumptuous sins"; we sin "with a high hand." People not only slip into sin and fall into sin; they rebel against the good and they rebel against God, and they sin on purpose. Touched by temptation and desire, they fan the flame, nurse and cherish their sins, and plan for their fruition. "There is no health in us."

In the clearest and most "natural" way then we are *used to* sin. We, therefore, never see it quite fully for what it is. Its heinousness is excused, explained or rationalized away. We like to think of it sometimes as part of our modernity, or our civilization; it makes us feel more sophisticated. But how does it look from God's viewpoint? This would be Jesus' perspective on it, of course, the reason for His coming at all, the reason for the Lamb slain from the foundation of the world, the reason for His great redemptive act, the reason for His setting His face "steadfastly to go to Jerusalem" knowing that the cross awaited Him there. But it is not in Gethsemane now a question of an intellectual understanding of the nature and reality of sin; it is now a question of experiencing it in Himself, feeling the unnatural shock at the very heart of His being. He is now to be the sin-bearer. What is called the "weight of sin" now falls on Him, smothers Him, staggers Him! The weight of that sin was the whole world's sin. Both Matthew and Mark tell us that He fell on the ground, fell on His face.

Analogies are not too helpful here because in our

human condition we cannot start with sinlessness and then "experience" sin for the first time. But we do have some hints and helps. We can picture the familiar problem of loving parents and a son who has gone wrong. Within limits then the parents have not sinned the sin of the son; at least with regard to his sin they are innocent. But this does not mean that they in a certain sense do not become bearers of his sin. Because of their love, because they can see better than he can what the sin has done and is doing to their beloved, the agony of his sin may be greater for them than for him. Innocent of his transgression they nevertheless bear the consequences of his transgression and suffer in many ways that he can neither see nor imagine. But the analogy breaks down both qualitatively and quantitatively when we really examine Jesus in the same sort of situation. Sinless in regard to any sin and every sin (qualitatively different) He bears the "sins of the whole world" (quantitatively different). The concept of all men's sins, everywhere and always, laid on Him is much too much for steady contemplation—"my soul," He said, "is exceeding sorrowful even unto death" (Matt. 26:38).

Another question with regard to the cup in Gethsemane has had little currency but really has great merit. Was the impact of the Gethsemane experience itself, apart from the expectancy of the cross later, so crushing that Jesus' prayers there were offered to save Him not from the cross later but from the Gethsemane experience itself. In that sense were not His prayers answered within the context of the garden? He "began to be greatly amazed" Mark tells us. The garden experience itself was much more than He had expected or different from what He had expected. Now in the present suffering, now in the overpowering experience of sin there in the garden, could it be that He would die of the shock right there and then? "Let *this* cup pass from me" was the prayer. Let me get through this Gethsemane experience that I may indeed move on to the cross. There had been His own great promise, "I, if I be lifted up from the earth, will draw all men unto me. This he said, signifying what death he should die" (John 12:33). But suppose He should die in the garden—"poor fellow, he must have had a heart attack"—would this be all there was to it? Where would be the promised lifting up, the redemptive act, the public witness "towering o'er the wrecks of time"? Here is indeed our Lord's great submission to the will of His Father, His perfect obedience again; if it is to be death in the garden "nevertheless not my will, but thine, be done" (Luke 22:42). No lifting up, no cross, no witness—but even this surprising turn of events must still be trusted to the Father's love and will, for even in this "God's hand is not shortened that he cannot save." His prayer was surely answered. There came an angel from heaven to strengthen Him (Luke 22:43). He went from the garden the calm and controlled person who dominated with spiritual power all the trials and persecutions which followed along the way to Golgotha. If there be merit in this interpretation then Gethsemane had no crying or cringing but a bearing of what was laid on Him at that moment and a prayer that the Gethsemane cup should pass that He might move on in God's will to the cross itself.

2

The Seven Last Words

It is relatively simple to observe and describe all the activity at the foot of the cross. But it is a different problem to discover what Jesus was doing on the cross itself. To understand at all we are limited to what He said, and what He said has been summed up in the seven last "words." Only by thinking on these have men had some clue to His inner experience.

I. "Father, forgive them; for they know not what they do" (Luke 23:34).

THESE WORDS ARE consistent with one of the most persistent themes of the New Testament: the wonder of forgiveness, amazing grace, what Paul Scherer has called "God's Unreason." The Apostle Paul urges us (Phil. 2:5) to "let this mind be in you" which was also in Christ Jesus, and any serious view of our most holy faith irresistibly forces us toward "the mind of Christ." It is a slant of mind, a total way of looking at things, a world view, a philosophy of life: "a different religion, a different world, a different way." Jesus speaks of Himself and His ministry as a "stumbling block" and adds, "blessed is he that findeth no occasion of stumbling in me." The Greek word for "stumbling block" is "scandalon"—

scandal. We can literally be "scandalized" by what Jesus says and does; Christ and His way cuts across our ordinary ways of thinking and doing; a new way of life has broken in and we are challenged and finally judged. What are we to do with the mind of Christ, His way of approaching reality?

Nothing judges us more quickly and surely than our Lord's view of forgiveness. For this great cause of redemption He had come. As is said in John's Gospel (3:17 RSV) "For God sent the Son into the world, not to condemn the world, but that the world might be saved through him." The whole thrust of His ministry is toward salvation; the whole method is forgiveness, and those who would follow the Master must, yes, must, forgive, and not just seven times but seventy times seven. This seems not only impossible but beyond our imagination, unless, of course, with a new birth and the formation of a new creature, we really have the mind of Christ. Students have frequently pointed out to me that the demands of the Sermon on the Mount, for example, are quite impossible; they are against human nature. One can answer only: "Indeed, they are against nature, our nature, but we are called to have a new nature; that's the whole point of our newness." Only when we are like Christ, or to the extent that we are like Christ, can we possibly obey Him, and only when we obey Him can we be like Him. And all this is most clearly illustrated when we are called upon to forgive.

How could Jesus have said these words of forgiveness

from the cross itself? But then how could Jesus not have said them? How impossible, yet how like Him. How impossible for us and yet how inescapable if we are to be like Him. In a situation where nothing like forgiveness would even be dreamed of, Jesus shows us that it is not only possible but is now the only necessity; and so He forgives. And at such a time one is shocked to remember that frightening prayer, "Forgive us our debts *as* we forgive our debtors." See where all this leaves us when we try to excuse ourselves for hardness of heart.

One of the struggles of Gethsemane, we recall, must have been over the impossibility of dying for the very ones who would bring Him to His death. And those who would crucify Him would be vulgar and crass, and heartless and cruel; the whole thing would go its relentless way without any sense or sensitivity. In the last analysis it would be done in ignorance and stupidity and there would be the rub. One could conceive, although with difficulty, some just sentence leading to capital punishment, and if the practice of the day demanded, leading even to crucifixion. But whatever other possible justifications, there is no justification for this. Think of what crowds, the sightseers, the soldiers, even those who merely looked and wondered, the passers-by were missing in their ignorance: a loving God, amazing grace, the cosmic reality of sin and now the cosmic act of redemption, and the one on the cross loving them with a broken heart. The stark cruelty coupled with the stark ignorance is just too much. Could He face all this? In the purity of His heart could He really forgive such people and give His life to accomplish their forgiveness? Gethsemane settled the issue; the cross exhibited the victory: love can cover sin.

The great Negro spiritual has great insight: "Were you there when they crucified my Lord?" It is a rhetorical question, for the answer is there all the time and every time. We were there; we are there. But just where are we? At the foot of the cross, blaspheming holy things, hardened against the one who loves us to the uttermost, going on in our rough-shod stupidity knowing not what we do: that is the terrible possibility. The only other possibility is that we are with Him, one with Him, united with Him in the fellowship of His sufferings, recognizing that in our Gethsemanes and our Golgothas a disciple is required to bear his own cross. With Christ's mind and heart we learn to forgive, really forgive, forgive at any cost even those, and especially those, who deserve no forgiveness. All is of grace. Blessed is he that findeth no occasion for stumbling in that.

II. "Truly, I say to you, today you will be with me in Paradise" (Luke 23:43 RSV).

These are the words of Jesus to the thief on the cross, His companion in the torture. These words are the great proof, the great apologetic, for they are the words of one dying man to another dying man; all secondary possibilities of human life and human hope have been stripped away. There is no place now, just humanly speaking, for evasion or subterfuge or figurative language, no place for fancy interpretations, no "fooling around." This is the final showdown; this is it. One does not enter here into discussions of various viewpoints, secondary authorities, or arguments about the situation or the existential options. Men generally accept the preeminent authority of Christ's teachings and His exhibition of the good life. However, men do argue about Christ's claims about Himself. Here is a claim about which men cannot argue for there is no other evidence from which to argue. Here is the end of the matter and one just knows that He knows; otherwise at such a time such a one as He is would have been silent. But He is not silent. Here His marvelous claims climax. He can make this astounding promise because even in the closing moments of His life He knows that with Him is life, the power of life over death, the assurance of Paradise with Him.

And how may the thief on the cross claim that Paradise? Only in penitence and faith. What a marvelous faith it is really. Although it is only the first step in faith, it is faith sufficient to the need. It is faith of the order of the mustard seed, but that much faith when it is true faith is enough. He could have turned to the soldiers: "Please, in mercy, take me down." He could have turned to the priests: "Please, in the name of all you know of love, in the name of your God, have mercy on me." He could have pleaded with the women, or with the crowd: "In the name of common humanity, save me from this; do something, this can't go on, a cross is unbearable." What an exercise in faith it is: the dying thief turns not to the victors but to the victim. He knows, as men have always known since, that there is no place to turn in suffering, or in absurdity and despair, in futility and hopelessness, except to the crucified one. "I, if I be lifted up, will draw all men." There is the expression of faith here in that revelation of Christ which comes in light and power from the Cross.

"Nothing in my hands I bring, simply to thy cross I cling:" so go the words of the old hymn. The penitent thief illustrates so clearly the least and the most that a man can finally do for his own salvation. "We contribute nothing finally to our own salvation but our own sins." We can only throw ourselves on God's mercy, His love released in grace through the satisfying redemptive act. The thief had never been nor could he ever be baptized, infant or adult, sprinkled or immersed. There could be no Eucharist however men might argue the real presence. He had no theology, no Christian education, no built-in tradition of Christian experience or cultural conditioning, no supporting liturgy, no practice of prayer. And surely there is no place here for the works of the law. The salvation of the thief on the cross brings us back to the grand simplicities of the faith, to the simple faith itself: trust in Jesus; whoever believes in Him shall be saved. Men in obedience, and for the sake of Christian faith and nature, must surely practice baptism and communion, engage in liturgy and prayers, practice holy living. But men are justified by faith and so have peace. It is all of grace and the dying thief seals the fact.

Strangely enough there is no social action here. It has been argued, and rightly, that Jesus had the power to save Himself. He could have responded in power to the taunts of those who said, "He saved others, himself he cannot save." He could have summoned "legions of angels." The other thief took this approach in his ravings: "Why don't you use your power and come down off the cross; why don't you use your power and get me off my cross?" Christ could have put His persecutors to rout. But this was the whole point: He emptied Himself and became obedient all the way to the cross. For this very cause He had come. "For us men and for our salvation" these things must needs come to pass. He simply could not save us except by refusing to use His powers to save Himself; thus He established the power of the cross itself. But there is still the question of why He did not save the two thieves from all this. Why not save the penitent thief; here if anywhere was an opportunity for social service, for the act of compassion, for the expression of humanitarian concern. But He did save him, and this we have lost sight of in our endless concern for social action and social service. As St. Theresa put it, "The soul of the care of the poor is the care of the poor soul." We keep forgetting that. Jesus took the thief to Paradise. That finally is what salvation is all about. The perspective is rightened; what is really relevant is made clear here.

Two other things demand some attention. First, Jesus did not reply to the taunts of His fiendish persecutors; He replied only to the call for mercy. This is His way. And the second is, that some needy people continue to criticize and judge when they should only cry for mercy. The second thief illustrates that the cross of salvation can also be the place of judgment.

III. "When Jesus saw his mother, and the disciple whom he loved standing near, he said to his mother, 'Woman, behold your son!' Then he said to the disciple, 'Behold your mother!' And from that hour the disciple took her to his own home" (John 19:26, 27 RSV).

Arthur John Gossip in his incomparable exposition of the Gospel according to John in the *Interpreter's Bible* (Vol. 8, p. 783) comments on this word from the cross sharing with us this simple quatrain attributed to C. A. Hall:

> Sow a thought and you reap an act.
> Sow an act, and you reap a habit.
> Sow a habit, and you reap a character.
> Sow a character, and you reap a destiny.

What Gossip makes of this is that Jesus' last act of thoughtfulness for His mother and His beloved disciple is expressive of His whole life as a man among men.

Love and loving habits are not the sort of things one suddenly thinks about at death; they are all of a piece with one's whole life. Nothing gives us greater insight into Jesus' day-to-day living than these tender last words. That brief satisfying description of His life, "He went about doing good," is here vividly and unforgettably portrayed in a moment. Little children had climbed into His lap, He was often the "man who came to dinner"—He was good company—He had lived His thirty years of preparation in the simple relationships of a laborer's home, He had surely been subject every day of His life to the needs and joys of human relationships. Paul in summing up the marks of decadent men says that they are "without natural affection" (Rom. 1:31) ("they lost all natural affection," says Phillips in his translation). One's "natural affection" is, therefore, a mark of goodness. This expression of natural affection is a mark of Jesus' good manliness; it can serve as a check on our own. **1717112**

But there is more here. When the children would have run to Jesus' arms it was the disciples who were offended by this and would have kept the children away—this Jesus is an important man, this teacher is a busy man, this Master has more important things to do than to play with children—so the disciples could have reasoned. Not so with our Lord, not so with the one whose life is filled with "natural affection." And how much more this whole approach to values is exhibited on the cross. In unspeakable agony of body and spirit He is now bearing the sins of the world, He is suffering neglect and disdain and cold heartlessness. His body and mind should have been turning in on Himself, He should have been tempted to self-pity, and surely His heart had been crying out for the pity of others. The destiny of all men everywhere and always was resting on His obedience and endurance all the way to the end. Yet here it is again, the mind of Christ, His new way against the expectancies of ordinary men. His mind was somehow lifted above Himself even now and in the midst of cross-bearing the lines of concern run not inward on Himself but outward to those who were bound to Him by the ties of natural affection. It is a healing truth as all truth is finally healing. It is good therapy, as Christ's way is always good therapy. There is a profound lesson here for us, and we are a long time in learning. Really thinking of others and their needs can help to make cross-bearing bearable.

As I write, one of the passing fancies of the day is Women's Liberation. Assuming for the sake of argument, that the problem is worth the fuss, can we see how involvement in such a program can mean neglect for husband or children? Mother is busy with something important and cannot be bothered with natural affection and the demands of the daily round. There are, of course, matters of great moment—race, war, poverty, ecology, sexuality—matters calling for and demanding our concern, our time, and our sacrifice. There are high callings, noble duties, and no man or woman can excuse himself from responsible action. Anyone of any maturity knows the insoluble problems which arise in judging between public demands and time for home and children. Indeed, the tensions are never finally and satisfactorially solved. Yet here in the revelations of the cross we see the one who never forgets His natural affections because His affections really are "natural," part of Him, part of His life, the natural outflow of His being. In such a life there will be sufficient time and proper place and wise choice. Love is the fulfillment of the law. One wonders here of John the Great Apostle on the Day of Judgment. Will he be able to face Jesus there and say to him, "I was so busy with large issues and great commissions that I neglected Mary." Well, hardly.

Why was Mary assigned to the care of John instead of to some other member of Mary's family? Because there is a unity in the cross which is greater than the unity of the family. Only as I am there and you are there are we really together, for the simple reason that we are both in the same place. Here some of the harsh demands and apparently paradoxical statements of Christ come clear. With what has been said about "natural affections," what can be said of "hating" members of one's family for the sake of Christ and His kingdom? This at least can be said and must be said: there is no possibility of "natural affection" among fallen men unless something of the cross is in that relationship. Thus we can only rightly love one another if we love Him first. "We love because he first loved us." When we are told in the Ten

Commandments that the "Lord our God is a jealous God" we naturally think that God being "jealous" must somehow be smallminded or fearful of the competition of other gods. Foolish thought! No, He is jealous because He is the Lover who cannot for love's sake look upon anyone or anything which will despoil His beloved, His loved ones. Therefore, our fullest felicity and the possibility of every good and happy relationship is bound up to our worship of Him. When He is put first all other things fall into their best and proper pattern. John and Mary, Tom, Dick and Harry, America and Russia, will find each other and find their natural relationships and affections only at the feet of the crucified one. Anything less will lead to confusion and futility.

Tertullian, the ancient church father, once said, "all that God does is marked by simplicity and power." The cross is God's mighty act and in the climax of that act He remembers the simplicities: "Behold thy son! . . . Behold thy mother!" Here indeed is Christlikeness.

IV. "I Thirst" (John 19:28).

Here is a human outcry, not so much a request as a simple affirmation, a cry we all understand. Every man has experienced some measure of this need and every man has suspected the far reaches to which this need can go. A few men have experienced thirst at the very end of human endurance which is what it is now for our Lord. We identify here in this word from the cross; we know how demanding the body can be. We are never purely spiritual, no self-discipline can carry a man beyond the final basic needs of the body. Christ was fully man and this cry is the inescapable cry of His very human flesh.

The brief and simple response is also human, humanity at its best. For someone was moved with compassion because he had basic human compassion in him. There was nothing to be done by those at the foot of the cross, no move to be made to stop or reverse the irresistible course of the cross event. Roman Law and Jewish Law had joined to put Jesus to death and there was no way to get it stopped, to pull out the nails, or bring rest to the pain-racked body. Only one thing could be done at this moment and it was done. One pauses hopefully to think of that one person and that one thing he could do and did do. The unknown compassionate one had to be of the priesthood or of the soldiery. We can speculate that he was a soldier because what he offered was the common drink always carried by soldiers. That one man: he did what he could out of compassion, for no other reason than the suffering of a fellow human being. Our hopes for that man rest on this: "When saw we thee athirst?" "As you did it unto one of the least of these my brothers, you did it to me." In his ignorance this simple soldier gave to Jesus Himself. One wonders what in Jesus' great compassion heaven will do with that gift.

Something must now be said of the legitimate de-

mands of the body even under the strictest asceticism,
even in the most devoted of cross-bearings. In the Sermon on the Mount Jesus says, "*When* you fast" and
then He tells us how to conduct ourselves at such a
time. The word is *when* you fast not *whether* you fast.
It seems to be His assumption that fasting, self-discipline, is a part of Christian discipleship. And men
have followed many disciplines in their attempts to
follow their Lord. But there is always the danger of
fasting just for the sake of fasting, "to be seen of men,"
as a religious exercise subtly tempting us to pride. And
so we can fast for the wrong reason. We can also go too
far, flogging and wrecking the body until it is no longer
a proper temple for the Holy Spirit. Under extreme
asceticism men can be driven to strangeness or even to
apparent insanity. In the strictest practice asceticism can
become a de-humanizing thing. Fasting must be for
something bigger than the fasting itself; self-discipline is
not an end in itself but is exercised to fit one for greater
ends; one lays aside the weights and the besetting sins in
order to run the race, and the race is the thing not the
fasting. We see this in Jesus who in the Father's will
could enjoy feast days and weddings and dinners out
and could still set His face toward the cross. We see it
now and in His words. He refused the doping of His
senses offered in the wine mingled with myrrh, for He
must bear suffering to the uttermost, but what He need
not suffer He would not suffer. Only one natural de-

mand of His physical body could be answered and His thirst was answered.

We are not to choose the disagreeable only because it is disagreeable but because it is part of the necessary path of duty to Christ. There must be both self-denial and denial of self, and this is right and sound for the sake of our high calling or the needs of others. All things can be sacrificed except principle, but not apart from principle. Pain for the sake of pain, torture for the sake of torture, is neither good nor Christlike. Some members of the early church gave sacrificial gifts to the common fund; we may suppose that Ananias and Sapphira did too. But they gave their sacrifices for the wrong reason and were struck dead. The cross was bad enough; Jesus did not have to make it worse. The calling was endurance at the point of duty but He did not dismiss the demands of the body just for the sake of discipline. Every demand is fulfilled only for the sake of the Father's will and for the demands of the redemptive act.

In a book called *His Decease at Jerusalem* the great Dutch theologian-statesman, Abraham Kuyper, supports the interesting thesis (pp. 246 ff.) that because thirst is so desperately aggravated by loss of blood—the wounded know this and the constant cry on the battlefield is for water—that we have here a continuum between Christ's blood sacrifice and His thirst. The cry bespeaks in another and vivid way the life which is being poured out. The thought is very suggestive and when one turns it around, all the hungering and thirsting of mankind finds response in the one who cried out "I thirst" as His blood was being shed for the remission of our sins. His insufficiency became our sufficiency.

V. "And about the ninth hour Jesus cried with a loud voice, 'Eli, Eli, lama sabach-thani?' that is, 'My God, my God, why hast thou forsaken me?' " (Matt. 27:46; Mark 15:34).

In the Matthew record we read "Eli, Eli" and in the Mark record "Eloi, Eloi"; the former is Hebrew, the latter is Aramaic.

No word from the cross is more baffling, for nothing in these words can be fully explained by language or logic. Here we are in the deeps. Our Lord is experiencing "Godforsakedness" and that is purely Hell and therefore basically irrational. We lack the understanding and the experience to follow Him here. We shudder at what the experience would be for us, and we worship in gratitude that it need not be our experience because He experienced it for us. We can only hear and ponder and wonder.

Sometimes preachers are tempted to dramatize and read or recite these words as they think Jesus might have said them. This simply will not do, but maybe the attempt to do so will be instructive. As a simple approach to the problem, just read the words aloud and try to determine where the emphasis should be. "*Why* hast thou forsaken me?" The Son of God, the Beloved of the Father, the one who has perfectly obeyed and lived in constant communion, this one altogether lovely and of good report, is forsaken by the Father who loves Him. Why? What kind of a Father can this be and what has happened here? How many of our own questionings of the ways of God are brought into this same arena of the soul's dark struggle?

Or should one read it with a different emphasis, "Why hast *thou* forsaken me?" In the midst of all this suffering at Golgotha surely there is one who cares. One is surely able to turn to the Father always in trust and hope; we can always count on those everlasting arms to bear us up. So one turns to God and God is not there; the heavens are brass. Our hope is built on hopelessness. Here is indeed "the dark night of the soul." Or try other emphases: "Why hast thou *forsaken* me?" or "Why hast thou forsaken *me*?" However we try to say it we have to say it every possible way and all ways together. In the clearest sense the words themselves are quite beyond us, as the experience itself is quite beyond us. The struggle here is our Lord's struggle. The cross for our salvation is the cross which only He can bear. Only the begotten of the Father is sufficient for these things. What He endured there only He could endure. We come to the edge of the abyss and cannot see, for here is the cost of sin, a cosmic struggle, and only the Lord's anointed can enter the fray with any hope of victory. Here the clash with demonic powers is finally measured. This is what our sin really is, and what it means, and what it takes to be cleansed and mastered.

Much is made here of the theological problem as related to the Father and the Son, their relationships, and God as one. We affirm that Christ is fully God and fully man, and yet just one person. We also affirm that God is one and that yet there are three persons in the Godhead: Father, Son, and Holy Spirit. We must not divide the essence nor confuse the persons. Neither can we speak of any division in the single personhood of Jesus Christ. He is God-man or man-God, but not God and man; He is not a mix of some sort. Who then in this cry of dereliction is crying to whom, and why must He cry when Paul assures us that "God was *in* Christ reconciling the world to himself?" All our explanations break down, our reasonings are lame, our solutions tend to solve the problem only by forgetting part of the problem. We are faced here, on the earth, at a given point in time, with the utter majesty and mystery of God the Almighty One, and all our categories of language and logic can serve only to clarify the problem, not clarify the answers. Luther once said that religion "is a man flat on his face." Christians would do well to prostrate themselves at the foot of the cross. Job was so sure that he would argue with God if he ever had a chance to face Him. He finally had his chance but Job had no arguments: "now my eye sees thee; therefore I despise myself, and repent in dust and ashes" (42:5, 6 RSV).

Christ is the revelation of God, the cross is the climax of
that revelation. The more we think we see and understand the more we are called upon to repent and to
worship.

But can we read only helplessness and hopelessness
out of this cry? No, there is more to think about. The
fact that the words are taken from Psalm 22 can lead in
another direction as we ponder all this. Jesus was master
of the Old Testament scriptures, and we know that they
formed His speech and supported His thoughts. One sees
this clearly, for example, in the temptation in the wil-
derness at the beginning of His ministry. It is not un-
usual, even today, for people in great moments of
anguish of spirit, to speak the words of the Bible to
sustain them, keeping the words of God at the center of
their thinking. Perhaps Jesus was reciting the whole
psalm and only part was heard by those at the cross,
only the first words, the opening words of the psalm.
There are other parallels to the cross experience in this
great psalm, "a company of evil-doers encircle me; they
have pierced my hands and feet." The psalm is replete
with such prophetic and suggestive words. But the
whole sweep of the psalm passes beyond complaint to
triumph (vv. 23-31) and there is this great word of
assurance: "he has not hid his face from him, but has
heard, when he cried to him" (v. 24c). Christ's cry of
loneliness and loss may well have moved through the
psalm to a prayer of assurance and deliverance. The
psalm in its entirety does not express any loss of faith in

God and we can believe Christ knew the whole psalm and used it all. In the experience of grief and bafflement, the experience of desertion, the depths of despair, at that very place He found His feet on the rock. Kierkegaarde goes so far as to suggest that only when the very deeps of despair are sounded, only then do we really cast ourselves on God in faith. This is faith: not on account of anything but in spite of everything. Christ's next word on the cross would seem to prove that this was His kind of faith.

VI. "Father, into thy hands I commend my spirit" (Luke 23:46).

The cry of dereliction, "Why hast thou forsaken me?" rests on Psalm 22 and we were led to believe that the best way to understand that cry is to read the whole psalm and see that Christ was using the psalm as a sustaining exercise in faith, and the whole psalm, one must recognize, is really a cry of faith out of the depths of despair. These next words from the cross apparently seal this interpretation, for immediately after the cry, which sounds by itself so finally hopeless, Christ puts Himself completely in His Father's hands. Luke tells us that He cried "with a loud voice" and His cry was this: "Into thy hands I commend my spirit." Many of the early church fathers interpret the "loud voice" as evidence of the fact that Christ died voluntarily. The cry now was not only a word of assurance; it was a shout of victory!

We are reminded of another great affirmation of faith. When His followers had turned away from Him in great numbers because He had challenged them with the "hard saying" about the bread of life (John 6:35ff.) Jesus posed the question to the twelve, "Will you also go away?" Peter's answer to the question is the answer of many of us in a variety of hard situations: "Lord, to whom shall we go? You have the words of eternal life." That puts the proposition very plainly: where indeed does one go? And men's hurts are healed very superficially if in their fears and sorrows they are not turned to their Father. "*Though* he slay me yet will I trust *him*," said Job in his despair.

Some years ago it was my privilege to accompany a great pastor as he ministered in a home where the beloved mother and wife had died. He had many comforting words to say and his own presence there was a comfort itself. But his last words were unforgettable and they were these: "Remember, she is in good hands." There it is; what else is there to say? On another plane of experience I remember fixing the wounded leg of my dog. There was some struggle and a hurt crying but he kept licking my hand. The hand of the one who was hurting him and the hand of the one who was healing him were the same, and his endurance of the one rested in his trust in the other. "Out of depths have I cried unto thee, O Lord." In this whole universe of endless space and cold and utter darkness, "To whom shall we go?" Could Jesus have turned to His friends and loved ones? None had fully understood and most had fled. But as in Paul's great hymn of faith (Rom. 8:28ff.), so here the words are fitting and powerful: "If God is for us, who is against us? . . . I am sure that neither death, nor life . . . .nor anything else in all creation, will be able to separate us from the love of God. . . ."

One writer has said of these words, "The darkness and desertion by God had passed and now a calmness returned." This won't do—and it helps our understanding to see why. First, it is unbelievable to think of "calmness" at any time on the cross and especially now in the death throes. Second, the cry of dereliction was not because of "desertion by God." Never! And this points up what must be said, and said again: it is in the very center of the experience of forsakenness that we find God. Finally and profoundly there is no other place to turn. Jeremy Taylor wrote a book called *Holy Living and Holy Dying*. The two are interlocked. In the last moments Jesus committed Himself to the one to whom He had constantly committed Himself all His days.

VII. "It is finished" (John 19:30).

These very last words are recorded only in John. They are quiet and touching. "It is finished," He said, and He bowed His head and gave up the ghost. It is as simple as that. "It is finished." Who can comprehend that "it?" The great preacher of Edinburgh, Alexander Whyte, was said to have preached forty sermons on John 3:16. One of the sermons was based on the simple word "so" in that well-known verse, "God *so* loved the world." God *so* loved; the possibilities of that little word seem endless. And in Jesus' last word, "It is finished" one's mind is forced back and back, to His every word and act, to His total purpose. One's thoughts are carried all the way back to the beginnings of things: God's eternal purpose, His decrees from all eternity, "the lamb slain from the foundation of the world." All such things are finished on the cross. This is the last act in the "finished work" of Jesus Christ.

It is a good exercise in understanding to read the Gospel accounts of Jesus Christ on two levels, and we recognize the two levels immediately in His name and title, Jesus, the Christ. On one level there is the story of a quiet modest family to whom a baby is born in Bethlehem. There is a growing boy in the village of Nazareth. There are the vicissitudes of an itinerant preacher and His followers. And there is the account of how this young preacher finally ran afoul the powers of the church and the state and was crucified by those who could not bear His words. But the story on the other level is probably the reason why the story is told at all. At the birth of that child the angels sang and His mother pondered many wonders in her heart. There had been a hint of divine understanding in the lad at the age of twelve; a descent of the Spirit on His entrance on His ministry. Marvelous powers had been exhibited; words of authority had come from His lips. There had been a transfiguration and strange phenomena in heaven and on earth had surrounded His crucifixion. Even the centurion who had seen many men die was led to witness at this death, "Truly this man was a son of God!" But more than such events was Jesus' own purpose expressed in His words, "No man takes my life from me, I lay it down of myself," and words to Pilate, "You would have no power over me unless it had been given you from above." In the intercessory prayer (high priestly prayer) recorded in John 17 are these words: "I glorified thee on earth, *having accomplished the work* which thou gavest me to do." And one may judge that this "accomplished work" is what was steadily His task and duty. Read His comments, for example, early in His ministry: "for the works which the Father has granted me, these very works which I am doing . . ." and one knows that Jesus looked on His whole life as that of accomplishing the Father's purpose in His life. "My meat and drink is to do the Father's will." The will is accomplished. "It is finished."

There is no end here of summations and speculations as to what the work was, and one's own slant on the Gospels is witnessed to in what one sees or emphasizes in that work. Whatever one chooses, however, there is still no end, for Christ came to reveal the Father and God is infinite, "my Father works until now and I work," and the work of Christ is the work of God. But some things are certain, even though they bring us to no end of possibilities, only to humble worship and greater expectation.

We get something of a lead from the "offices" of Christ on which historically and classically the theologians and churchmen have settled: Christ was (and is) prophet, priest, and king, and in each office He shows us not one but two things. As prophet He not only speaks "the wonderful words of life," but He also displays Himself as the living word; as king He is not only the one who rightfully rules and commands but He also commands and rules as the suffering servant, the one who came "not to be ministered unto but to minister and to give his life a ransom . . . ." Finally, and preeminently He is priest, for He came to the climax of His ministry on the cross, the offering up of a sacrifice of life and the pouring out of blood. Christ as priest is both the offerer and the offering, the priest who is also the sacrifice. He laid down His own life, and in that act "It is finished." That finished work is, as the great creed affirms, "For us men and for our salvation."

The last moment then is a moment of completion and of victory. Gustaf Aulen wrote a great book entitled *Christus Victor* which underlines very well just one view of the atonement. But the title has significance for every view of the atonement. The victim, as John Whale has suggested, is the victor. Medieval art, of which there was much and which has too much dominated our thinking on holy things, usually portrayed Christ on the cross in pathos and defeat. But the early church fathers had a surer instinct. The suffering of Christ is in no way minimized, but in their art Christ on the cross wears a crown. "Towering o'er the wrecks of time" the cross reveals the *reigning* Christ. " . . . I lay down my life, that I may take it again. No one takes it from me, but I lay it down of my own accord. I have power to lay it down, and I have power to take it again" (John 10:17, 18 RSV). There will come now a resurrection. The power of life and love over death and sin is the power of the cross.

The Disciples' Way

"But Jesus answered, 'You do not know what you are asking. Are you able to drink the cup that I am to drink?' They said to him, 'We are able.' He said to them, 'You will drink my cup' " (Matthew 20:22, 23 RSV).

IT APPEARS that we are here in the presence of presumption compounded. There is the presumption of the mother of James and John. What a strange story it seems to us now. Jesus had just taken the twelve disciples aside to forewarn them of what should befall Him when they arrived in Jerusalem. He was to be arrested, condemned to death, delivered up to be crucified. That He was to be "raised the third day," was added, and that idea may or may not have been taken seriously or understood clearly. The evidence in the later accounts seems to indicate that any understanding the disciples may have had of a resurrection was not firm enough to hold them fast during the trials, or at the cross, or during the three days of Jesus in the tomb. It goes without saying then that under the circumstances the request of the mother for her sons, that they should sit "one on your right hand and one on your left in your kingdom" is a very strange one. What kingdom? What kind of a kingdom? What status could she possibly wish for her sons when the leader Himself had just announced His own crucifixion? But if she and her sons were sensing something of our Lord's resurrection power and glory, then the request is not only presumptuous, it is utterly selfish. And how can one justify such selfishness in the presence of the one whose next move in the kingdom enterprise is to be marked by utter and complete selflessness, self-giving to the end? How does one make a bid for power in a kingdom which is to be established by way of a cross?

It is no wonder that Jesus, with characteristic good manners and tenderness, has to answer at first, "You do not know what you are asking." And, of course, they didn't. The scene brings to mind His prayer later on the cross, "Father, forgive them; for they know not what they do." As the conversation developed it turned out that what they were asking was not in Jesus' power to grant, but in any case He had to make clear to them that even to accompany Him in His kingdom enterprise required that they go with Him on the way of the cross. "If any man would come after me, let him deny himself and take up his cross and follow me." To follow Christ is to bear a cross; there is no such thing as crossless Christianity.

So Jesus put the question plainly: "Are you able to drink the cup that I am to drink?" Foreshadowed in these words are Gethsemane and Golgotha.

Now comes the second act of presumption, the confidence with which James and John responded, "We are able." How could they possibly have said a thing like that? "They know not what they do." Again we remember that Jesus had just said before this conversation began that He must be arrested and delivered up to be "mocked and scourged and crucified." And we know from Gethsemane and the words from the cross how far and how deep a cross experience can go. Yet the impression given here is one of glibness, almost cheapness. Are you able to drink the cup? Sure! It is bad enough for them to have asked for the seats of honor in the kingdom, but now this: the brash, superficial (blasphemous?) judgment of what Christ's drinking of the cup will mean for Him, and what little, apparently, it will mean to them. And these men were of "The Twelve," James and John of the "Inner Three"; James and John the Apostles, St. James, St. John. How far away even these followers are from the truth in Christ.

So our criticisms of these two come easily, come easily that is until we remember again that "with what judgment you pronounce you will be judged." Psychologists like to assure us that judgment of others is so often self-judgment. The judgment on James and John for their overconfidence, their lack of sensitivity and understanding, turns easily and immediately on ourselves. Think for just a moment of how you "joined church." If your experience was like mine you were probably disappointed at the time that the whole process was so routine and easy. If certain questions were put to you they were probably read quickly from a book, or some "elder" with some embarrassment for his public assignment and his intrusion into your private life, hesitantly posed a question or two. There was probably some free prayer, hand-shaking all around, and a sense of relief when the "exercise" or "rite" was all over. So you joined up. But just what did you join up to: "co-workers with Him," or the "fellowship of His sufferings," or membership in a body, the "body of Christ" where when one suffers "all suffer"? If the question had been rightly put the question had to be "Are you able to drink the cup?" Now think of our own glib answers and how easily we said, "We are able."

Going back to our consideration of the cup which Jesus prayed about in the garden, we have to face the cup ourselves; to be a member of the church is to have affirmed, as James and John did, "We are able." What then of the *physical suffering*, that part of the cup which we have said we are able to drink? In the American scene there is not much of this for anyone unless one counts what happens to certain social action groups, who, in the name of Christ, have suffered because of the draft, or race, or in taking a stand on poverty, or injustice. In such matters the end is not yet, but as things now stand very few church "members" are found in such involvements. The time may not be too far distant when martyrdom—on *either* side of such issues, if you like—will be more widespread than we can now picture. On the world scene, however, the body of Christ is being harassed in such ways and with such continuity as would have marked the most vicious martyrdoms of the early church. "More people have suffered for their faith in the last thirty years than in the whole history of the Christian Church." So a church historian reported recently. How he could support such figures it is hard to say, but at least they remind us of Christians in Russia and China (What was done to all those wonderful Chinese Christians?), in Africa, especially in the Sudan, in some countries in South America. The news media touch the matter lightly because they do not know how to handle religion except in a sentimental way. However, numerous church periodicals, if read closely, amaze one with the totals of those persecuted month after month. The North American continent seems, on the whole, to be spared now, a kind of island of security in a sea of persecution. As Christians, however, two things must be said about the cup of physical suffering for every Christian: (1) Such suffering must be looked upon as a clear option and constant potential in the acceptance of Christ; one cannot join the body of the crucified one and deny this kind of built-in possibility, and (2) insofar as we are members of the body, live and sensitive members of that body, we are called upon to suffer when the body suffers. When the body hurts at any point or in any member, the whole body suffers. That we find ourselves incapable of any such hurt may merely be indicative of the fact that we don't really belong! But we did say, didn't we, when we "joined church" that we do belong. Maybe we want to reconsider, because Christ always warned any would-be followers to count the cost.

Christ's cup and our cup also mean *mental suffering*, mental anguish. It is here perhaps that Christians of the West can most clearly see how it stands with them. We evade such participation like the plague. With regard to our Christian commitments and affirmations we not only will not accept mental suffering, despising the shame, facing the "scandal" of our position but also we can't face even mild embarrassment. We are like Peter warming himself at the fire; the questionings of a little servant girl, the skepticism or cynicism of nobodies, drive us to denials of our Lord. Christianity does not lose ground so much because people solidly deny their faith but because those called upon to speak a word for Christ remain silent. Public opinion is powerful, but only when the opinion is made public. The shameful retreat is a mark of Christian non-witness in our day and in our culture. We simply will not face up, stand up, or be counted. If Christ or Christ's way are ever live options in a business deal, or a community decision, or an educational philosophy, one would never recognize the fact from any witness which Christians express. The Lord's name can be blasphemed at a bridge party or at the bowling league or at an easy-going luncheon, and we look and listen in vain for any counter-witness from a Christian. More and more Christianity is driven into and confined within the safe walls of a church building, and it all moves out into the "world" with great care and hesitancy. And why? Because Christians fail to recognize or accept that when they said that they were able to drink the cup they chose that part of the cup. Jesus in the garden and on the cross "despised the shame." We know it is a coward's way and a denial of our confessed faith, this failure to accept the cup, because we will not despise the shame.

From the physical to the mental, and then to the deeps, the dregs, thus we move in the acceptance of the cup. Remember how it was with our Lord; the last struggle was a *soul* struggle when He began to bear the sins of others. So it must be with us. In following our Lord we must become sin-bearers. He bore the sins of many; we must at least endure the sins of some. From this demand of our faith we recoil. Christ's sinlessness made His sin-bearing particularly excruciating. We cannot plead His purity for ourselves. But there are sinners and sins around us which seem to be beyond our tolerance, things we cannot face, cannot stomach, things we never do and cannot imagine others doing, people and people's ways we cannot stand. We want no part in their need for redemption: our grace just runs out. Our natural inclination, therefore, is to withdraw. Most scholars have agreed that monasteries began because men could not see how they could possibly practice their Christian faith in a very sinful world. So they withdrew. We must put proper value on their faithful prayers and their careful preservation of learning in their monasteries. We must believe in and support such efforts toward holiness of life and recognize such values even in this materialistic age. We can understand such a vocation, such a "calling." But with the Reformation, Calvin and Luther brought the Christian calling back into the world. A Christian is "called" to exercise his vocation in the midst of men and affairs. He is "called" in his place of employment, in the demands of his citizenship, and certainly in his marriage and family. In such activities, however, he loses the protection and security of his private devotional life. The care of his own soul becomes increasingly precarious.

The transfiguration experience of the disciples with Jesus illustrates this temptation to withdraw. It was Peter who expressed the desire that they should build tabernacles on that mount, places of abode where godliness could be clearly seen and experienced. It was Jesus, and typically Jesus, who led them down the mountain again. Their very first experience after the transfiguration was with the demonic. They were forced from the "mountain-top experience" into the sinfulness of the "world." The transfiguration experiences feed and inspire us but only to increase our concern for others and to enrich our service to them, all for Christ's sake. In the hurly-burly of daily living our purity and holiness may be badly discolored, nevertheless, it is there where our true Christianity must be brought to bear on all of life. This is all part of what we constantly see in Christ's incarnation. He emptied Himself and became obedient all the way to the cross. So also we must arrive at that point on the battlefield of the soul where against all our own desires for evasion or escape we finally say, "Not my will, but thine be done," and walk out to work our own work of redemption, bearing the cross laid on us.

One final word is called for in the light of the suggestion made when discussing Jesus' experience in Gethsemane. That suggestion was that the struggle in the garden, not the cross before Him was the cup from which Jesus was praying for deliverance. Gethsemane itself might have destroyed Him in the breaking burden of sin which He began there to endure. What then would become of His witness on the cross, the redeeming act toward which His whole life had been moving? The situation and the concern are the same for us. We have certain expectancies in our own self-giving, things that we long to see happen from our own sacrifices. Sometimes, being human, we might want reward or recognition for our own special kind of martyrdom. Suppose no one sees, suppose no one understands, suppose there is no record, and nothing is accomplished. In such a situation more than anywhere else we can be tempted to evade the cup, find some other way, or even a way out. This may well be the greatest venture of our faith, to lay all on the altar of our sacrificial obedience and even allow our noblest hopes and greatest sacrifices to come to naught, resting only in the Father's over-ruling, wise, and loving providence.

4

The Problem of Identity

Meditate on the cross to find in imagination our identity there with the victim, our recognition that this is our sin which crucifies the Lord of Life afresh, our acceptance of what has been done for us, and our repentance unto newness of life. It is our identity with that sacrifice which will lead to our fitness for service. Thus in the fellowship of His suffering we are fitted to bear our own cross in our service for others.

SOME YEARS AGO in Egypt I was taken along the coast of the Mediterranean some miles east of Alexandria and shown the place and told the circumstances of a tragic double drowning. There is a ragged and rocky point on the shoreline where the sea currents run in a troubled and treacherous way and swimmers are warned to stay away. A young Egyptian girl had been caught there and was being washed out to sea when two young men, missionaries, swam out after her. In an unbelievable and bizarre combination of circumstances the girl was rescued but the two men who rescued her were washed out to sea and drowned.

It was a strange thing, the sort of thing one ponders about for a long time and many times thereafter. One wonders about that girl. How does it feel to live one's life knowing all the time that you live only because some others, in this case two men in the prime of life, have given up their lives in order that you may live. One can guess what a tremendous motive this could be for worthy living. At such a price one could not help but give his best and give it constantly; there would be no way ever to tell whether one had lived to the full for such a sacrifice. Later I inquired about the girl and found that she had reached full womanhood now. But what a disappointment! Her life has counted for nothing. She became fat, indifferent, and lazy. Humanly speaking, and from one's own limited viewpoint, the whole sacrifice had been in vain. One could level on the girl's life nothing but condemnation. She had not only wasted the one life she had but she had also wasted the lives of two others who had died that she might live.

One of my favorite baseball players was Don Hoak who played third base for the Pittsburgh Pirates. Apart from his evident skills his play was marked by great drive and intensity. He literally gave everything he had and that constantly. He was one of the most dedicated athletes I have ever seen. I never had a chance to meet him but did know a friend of his and we often spoke of Don Hoak. And, of course, we spoke of his characteristic intensity. My friend often went hunting with him and told me that on a hunting trip Don was the same way. He walked fast, always on the alert, pursued the game tirelessly, completely dedicated to the thing at hand, this time hunting rather than baseball. This dedication was the mark of his life. And why? Well, as my friend reported, Don had been in military service and experienced the death of his brother, killed in action as they moved forward in battle side by side. From that day Don Hoak decided that he had two lives to lead; he must live his own life and in some indefineable way try to live a life for his brother also.

We wonder about the two cases and what made the difference. It is probably unjust to have expected too much from the Egyptian girl. It was too much to expect that she could appreciate or absorb what had been done for her. She may have been slow of mind or heart. All of us lack something in imagination, and so she could not grasp what had happened. Not knowing the men who had died for her she could hardly have identified with them in any emotional way. Maybe she tried to understand; maybe she tried to picture the whole thing clearly. The fact of the matter is that she could not. What had happened *for* her never happened *to* her so nothing happened *in* her. What should have motivated her from the heart of her life never found lodgment in her heart. In the case of the ballplayer, Don Hoak, the death of his brother was not only an immediate and vivid experience, shocking in its proximity, but it was his brother. The emotional ties were of the very stuff of his life from the experiences of their boyhood together to their fellowship in fear in the heart of battle. It is enough to say that the reality of identity in this case needed no urging from anyone on the outside. Imagination was quick and clear thoughout the rest of Don's life.

Meditation on the cross of Christ is urged upon us periodically as the calendar of the church year moves along, and we make the effort, some of us quite spasmodically and some of us in puzzlement or ignorance. What are we supposed to do? What is supposed to happen? Just this. The purpose of meditation is so to stir up our imaginations that we can indeed identify with the cross experience. Christ died for our sins. That means my sins, today's sins, this sin. Thus when we "accept Christ" we not only accept Him for what He is but we also have to accept His view of our sin, His definition of the desperation of our need (we really are lost without Him). We also must accept what He has had to do about sin, what the cost was and is. It is His life given for our lives, "the iniquity of us all" was laid on Him. He "became sin for us," and it is certainly true that "with his stripes we are healed." Like the girl or the ballplayer we either can or we cannot identify; in the one case we go along as if nothing ever happened and certainly never happened for us; in the other case we are forced to live a life and a full life for Christ's sake. Thus we hear the message and it is good news—we are saved. We can memorize the message, even repeat it to others, and we can know in our heads that the thing happened. But from the head to the heart? Ah, there's the problem. He is ours and we are His; it is an affair of the heart, of the emotions, of the wellsprings of life. And until and unless this has happened, nothing has happened for us. We are something like that poor girl who illustrated by her whole life that she had nothing but careless disdain for the greatest thing that was ever done for her.

We are called to meditate on the cross. Not only are we called so to do; it is the very stuff of our Christian life. This is why such meditation has been so much the activity of the saints. This is why some attempted to do nothing else. This is why we ourselves, even with the thinness and superficiality of much of our Christian living, recognize what such little meditation has done for us when we have given it the time and effort. This is why in our reading of the events we must bring to bear on such reading all the powers of our intelligence and especially our imaginations to find ourselves there, at the foot of the cross; sensing the shock to Him which must in some measure become the shock to us, so that we can go away from the experience not only knowing that all this was for our sakes but also discovering in the experience the new motivation for life. It is one of the activities of the Holy Spirit to take of the things of Christ and show them to us. In prayer and meditation there is room for the Spirit's work; the things of Christ give us the cross experience and then newness of life.

In the Old Testament where we find the first instructions in these things it is interesting to see what place is given to this matter of imagination and identity. In the Book of Leviticus where there is given close and formal instruction for the great and complex sacrificial system—pointing toward the necessity of the cross and toward the nature of the cross—it is significant that in

the directions for sacrifice man is called upon to identify with the victim. It is not merely a question of the
value or the cost of the thing sacrificed; it is much more
than that. Just begin leafing through the opening chap-
ters of Leviticus and see how often it is repeated that
the one making his sacrifice must have his hand on the
victim while the sacrifice takes place. One is really *there*
when the sacrifice takes place.

The Israelites were required to bring the best that
they had and again this represented not only cost or
market-value but the care one had to take from day-to-
day to preserve this grain or this animal in the greatest
purity possible. There was necessarily, therefore, great
identity already involved, the kind of satisfaction one
takes in other creative fields when he has done a piece
of woodwork or when she has brought out some needle-
work to show to a friend. One has given of one's self
creatively and for that very reason, personally.

Think a little of how one went about preparing a
lamb or a kid "without blemish." The little animal
would be a virtual pet in the home, fed in a special way,
protected, cleansed; it is easy to imagine how the animal
was readied. Now the poor little, helpless beast is laid
out on the altar and one must hold his hand on the
quivering body while the priest cuts its throat. Let your
imagination run. Could you really do it? Could you ever
do it easily? I think not. And so many thoughts would
run through your head. Is all this necessary? Is the
whole thing all that bad? It all seems such a shame,

somehow. And it is! Without the shedding of blood there is no remission of sin and you can begin to believe how heinous your whole sin life is as you keep your hand on the lamb's body while he dies for your cleansing. It isn't hard to imagine how moving all this would be and how a man would be brought up short about his whole business of easy sinning. We find it easy to sentimentalize about animals in our society today and perhaps put too much into such an event. But in the cross of Christ there is a man dying, one altogether lovely, surely the lamb without blemish. And He is ours and we are His—we did accept Him did we not? What now of our sense of sin, our shuddering revulsion against all that requires the death of the Lord of Life? This is the Beloved Son yet He dies for us. And God Himself was there for God was in Christ reconciling the world to Himself. Is all this for you? If it is and if you can think about it imaginatively for even a short while it will make all the difference in the world—it does make all the difference in the world!

Several times in my life I have hit a small animal on the highway. It is always the same kind of experience, just a slight shudder of the car, a kind of soft thumping sound. There has never been any outcry that I have ever heard. But there it all is, done, finished. One does not labor the point here that this death was in any way for me, although something of my own carelessness or speed may have contributed to the death of that helpless little thing. What does affect me in such an experience, however, is this: I cannot shake it for a long, long time afterward. I am led to think of life and death, the strangeness and the completeness of death as over against life. Again it is meditation, imagination; the shudder that goes through me is real identity. How is it then that I find it so easy to read about, think about, and then dismiss the whole cross event. One must not, you know; it is a matter of life and death. Again, meditate on the cross.

P. T. Forsyth, that great theologian of the cross, tells of an experience in a large prep school where there was a great headmaster. The headmaster had been away for a short while and rebellion had broken out in the school. Things had been broken and the morale of the school was in disarray. On his return he called an assembly of the whole student body. In their presence he laid out a thick ruler and then called for the president of the student body to come to the platform to represent the student body. The young man came to the platform rebellious and sullen, knowing that he would receive some punishment for the school. He was tightened up and ready to fight. But when he stood before the headmaster he was completely unmanned by what the headmaster said. "All sin leads to suffering. Someone has sinned here and the sin is against our whole life together. One of us must suffer. I choose to suffer for that sin." He handed the ruler to the boy, held out his hand, and commanded the boy to beat that hand. The boy in his confusion and shame refused to turn against his master. So the master seized the ruler and beat upon the palm of his own hand until the blood came. Then he held the bloody hand up for all to see. They saw the bloody hand, they saw what they had done, in tears they came, begging forgiveness. What do we have to see at the cross to understand, to accept, to repent, to live life anew?

The Cup of Remembrance

This Cup *provides meditation for Holy Week as we think of that death for us then and now. But we know one more thing now. He died for our sins but was raised for our justification. We stand rightened before God because of the cross but in the power of the resurrection. Now we live daily in that light and that hope. We are called now to be "heirs of God and joint heirs with Jesus Christ," everything in the universe ours because of Him. "Eye hath not seen nor has it entered into the heart of man" what has been prepared for His children. It will be bliss beyond compare; we enter into glory.*

MARTIN LUTHER is well known as the initiator of the Protestant Reformation in the sixteenth century. Another reformer of the same period was Ulrich Zwingli. These two men met early in that century at Marburg and had a terrible argument over the Lord's Supper, an argument which split the German and Swiss churches in such a way and with such finality that the breech has not yet been healed. What they were arguing about was the manner of the Lord's presence in the Lord's Supper. Luther argued for the literal interpretation of the words "This is my body . . . this is my blood." He held that the word "is" in some fashion meant a kind of equation. The Roman Catholics had maintained that in the miracle of the Mass the bread and the wine miraculously become the very body and blood of Christ. Luther thought this led to idolatry but he still wanted to give the proper weight to the word "is" (probably to protect the literal authority of the Scriptures at that point) and so he insisted that at the communion the body and blood of Christ are "in, around, and under" the elements of bread and wine so that when one partakes of the elements he really at the same time literally takes Christ's body and blood. Zwingli did not meet this argument straight on but insisted that the important words in the institution of the supper are, "This do in remembrance of me." He made out of the supper simply a memorial feast. The key word for him was "remembrance."

John Calvin's approach was to insist that the communion is remembrance but more than remembrance, and that there is the real presence of our Lord at communion, but not a physical presence. Christ is *really* present but not in any physical sense, and that real, spiritual presence is available to the believer in his response in faith. What has to happen at the Lord's Supper is a communion between the believer and his Lord, for the believer's blessing and nurture, and this is possible according to our Lord's promise and according to our faith. Believer and Lord meet and commune and one does indeed gain sustenance from "the broken body and shed blood" of the Saviour. This view is not to minimize the mystery of the miracle of what takes place, for as Calvin says, "No person may measure the sublimity of the subject." Or again, "Nothing remains, therefore, but to break forth in admiration of that mystery, which his mind is as unable to understand as his tongue to express." It is not necessary, therefore, to think of the miracle as something less than the Roman Catholics maintain but to understand the nature of the miracle that takes place.

Bringing to mind what has been said thus far in this volume the move has been from Old Testament beginnings to the Gethsemane experience, to the cross, to the disciples' road. Now the question is, how all this which has been done, in some sense still is being done, being experienced week after week in churches all across the world as Christians meet around the Lord's table in obedience to His command, "This do in remembrance of me," how is the observance of the death of Christ in the first century the means by which Christians participate in His body and blood in this century? How are all the benefits of our Lord's cup the nourishment of the present moment? How does a Christian grow and become strong now by "eating and drinking" His body and blood?

To get at this one must understand several things. The understanding is not easy and requires thought and meditation. What is suggested here is very brief and should serve only as a series of guidelines for anyone who faces his holy faith seriously, for all this has been the substance of theological thought for the whole history of the church.

One must first think about eternity and time. God dwells in all eternity, in the eternal now, and we human beings move step by step through our moments in time. How this can be is a question for the philosophers, but we do know from the Scriptures that the death of Christ which occurred in time, in a certain place, and among men, was an expression of the eternal fact that the Lamb had been slain "from the foundation of the world." And when we come to the Book of Revelation we discover that the victory of God through Christ over the forces of Satan is already accomplished. We speak correctly about the "finished work" of Christ. There is, for example, something called "humanity" and as we come along in time, one by one, we take on this thing called "humanity" during our sojourn on earth. So with Christ and all His benefits. What happened on the cross happens now and when we drink the cup we are participating in Christ's cup in the garden and on the cross. The writer to the Hebrews describes our Lord as "Jesus Christ, the same, yesterday, today and forever." This is not just a description of Christ's everlastingness but assures us that Christ in the believer's heart is the same now as He was for the first believers. Thus when Paul says "It is no longer I that live but Christ liveth in me," or again, "For me to live is Christ," he not only is describing his own experience but the experience of every believer since. When we come to the table of our Lord we are participating in the "eternal now" not only of the universal Christ but the eternal cosmic Christ. What Christ did He does; it is Christ in us—now!—"the hope of glory." It is not only possible but necessary therefore to understand that the Lord is with the believers at the Lord's table now as He was in the upper room.

We must also understand the nature of symbolism if we are to grasp the reality of what takes place when we drink the cup. Symbols are much more than just an easy representation, one thing standing for another. A true symbol not only illustrates something else but must also convey something else. The church fathers have talked about the symbolism in the Lord's Supper by describing the elements, the bread and the cup, as "physical signs of spiritual realities," or "external signs of interior realities." What they are saying is that when one gets hold of the physical signs, these signs convey or communicate realities as well as outward forms. An American flag is made up of a certain amount of goods on which a certain monetary value is placed. There is a sense in which one can say that the flag is "only" so much material. Why then do we stand at attention, or doff our hats, or hold our hands over our hearts in the presence of the passing flag? Why would we react violently to someone who would violate the flag? The answer is simple: the physical sign not only stands for but also carries and contains a great unseen, spiritual reality. One reads a map and says, "This is Route 128, and this is the turnpike, and this is the freeway," but no one drives his car on the roads on the map. As C. S. Lewis has pointed out, we cannot take the trip without the map but one never confuses the map with the trip. One sees tears on the face of a child. "There is sadness," we say. But where is the sadness? Not in the tears surely. But when we see the physical sign, the tears, we know that the sadness is there. This is true symbolism: when the physical sign is there we know that the invisible reality is there.

Thus in the Lord's Supper the cup of blessing does indeed carry the blessing. The bread stands for the broken body, the cup stands for the shed blood, but in communion the broken body and shed blood are "really" not "physically" present. The signs communicate the reality. Christ is truly present. This is why "remembrance" is not enough. There has to be a happening and one must "discern" the Lord's body as Paul warns. That a person has to mature spiritually and grow in this experience is surely evident on the face of it. A child can tear up a flag with impunity, but an adult cannot; one who has suffered for the flag experiences greater reality than one who has kept the whole experience at arm's length. Again, one must discipline himself to meditate on these things.

The question is often raised why one needs the elements of the Lord's Supper when Christ is always present with the believer. We need to remind ourselves that we are physical beings and need physical things as channels of meaning and reality. Although "spiritual things are spiritually discerned" the discernment is mediated by physical things. To stop at the sign is idolatry; we worship the creature rather than the Creator. The

heavens declare the glory of God but we worship not
the heavens but the God who is declared by the heavens.
There are "visible words" as well as spoken words and
whereas the good news of the gospel is spoken to us and
our lives are changed, it is also true that the gospel is set
before us visibly in the sacrament and on this too we
feed. We need the signs, not because Christ is not always
present with us, but to "bring to remembrance," to
bring into focus, to intensify. It is not an experience
different in kind but different in thrust. We are surrounded by the sunlight, but a curved glass can bring
that sunlight to bear on a direct point in time and place,
and at that point, there is enough intensity to bring a
piece of paper into flame. Something lights up, comes
alive in a new way. So with the Supper. We need feast
days, fast days, anniversaries, gifts, acts of love, and our
Father knows that we need the signs of the bread and
the cup to bring to remembrance, to bring into sharp
focus and experience, what we have sensed in general in
the presence of Christ in our lives. A girl does not wear
an engagement ring to tell her that a man loves her, but
when she really looks at the ring from time to time, the
great reality of his love comes flooding in and she is
assured and renewed. The finished work of Calvary is
experienced afresh and decisively at the Lord's Supper,
in the act of remembrance.

This is the nature, therefore, of "remembrance." A
very appealing story which is also instructive, concerns a
young man who was called into military service. His

father was deeply concerned and wanted to do what he could. He would have replaced his boy if it had been at all possible. He would have gone with him and protected him from danger if that had been at all possible. But there was really nothing he could do. The boy was being taken away from him entirely, into unknown places and into great danger. He offered the young man a blank check to cover any possible contingency and assured the young man that he could call anytime and the father would "cover" whatever his need might be. The young man could see nothing worthwhile in all this, although he appreciated what his father was trying to do. Finally the father asked him, "What can I do, what can I give you?" The boy replied, "Please give me your pocketknife." Why that? Because the father had a characteristic habit of taking out his pocket-knife and turning it over and over in his hand while thinking or talking. The little habit was part of him. So the boy took the knife. In times of loneliness or fear, and especially in times of temptation, he took out the knife, turned it over in his hand as he had seen his father doing, and as he held onto this physical sign there was brought to vivid remembrance all that his father stood for, all his home and family meant to him, and for brief moments he communed with his father and his family. The sign was not just a memory of something else but a means by which that something else came and lodged in his mind and heart.

On the night in which Jesus was betrayed He told His disciples, as they looked at the bread and the wine and tried to understand what was transpiring in the life of their beloved leader, "This do in remembrance of me." In obedience to that command men everywhere have had their feast of remembrance and communed with their Lord. The tragic event on Calvary's hill was of eternal and cosmic significance as eternity broke into time in the final act of redemption. And that break into time is still the Christ-event at the Lord's table. Those who gather in obedience, who discern the Lord's body in the visible word, who take symbolically what communicates the great reality, have that remembrance which communicates His broken body and shed blood and all the blessings of nurture and renewal and redemption which the crucified Lord has for His children who believe.